IMAGINEUS,THESWARM

IMAGINE US, THE SWARM

Muriel Leung

Nightboat Books   New York

ISBN: 978-1-64362-073-2

Cover Art by Muriel Leung
Design and typesetting by Rissa Hochberger
Typeset in JJannon and Didot

Cataloging-in-publication data is available
from the Library of Congress

Nightboat Books
New York
www.nightboat.org

CONTENTS

To Susan Hammoudeh

THIS IS TO LIVE SEVERAL LIVES

....

....

Once, when I was very, very young,
I studied the curious lives of bees

their steadfast and synchronous labor

thinking of what it means
to be at once [a colony] and [alone].

....

....

....

....

A bee learns to become a Müllerian mimic, dressed as some other creature with a deadlier poison.

`

....

A bee who is sometimes [a wasp], sometimes [a stinging beetle], sometimes larger than its small [self].

....
....
....

Each one working so hard to perform a sense of safety..
....
....
....
....
....
....

Some nights, I am thinking of the colony of my father and me and what the bees know to be true.

....
....
....

To survive a history in the wild requires
arduous labor of some effortlessly seeming
toil as in

....
....
....

I want to tell you about his commute.
He smelled like leather and tobacco.
He was a type of burning.
He said "Yes" often.
The restaurant was a hole he fell into.
Most nights, I waited for him.
When he was home.
He was tired.
That's all.

....
....
....

Maybe I'm making this up. I can't remember. I asked my father once, "Do you ever get lonely?" Did he answer?

……………………………………………………

……………………………………………………

……………………………………………………

……………………………………………………

……………………………………………………

……………………………………………………

……………………………………………………

I set out to write a book about [   ] but it was about [   ] instead. After he died, [   ] was all that was left.

......................................Let me posit this now..the book.................

....a labor.............................a means to measure...

....

.....................................the contradictions of one's [life] against [another].................

....

....

He wrote to me in a letter...

....

....

..............................."You have to work hard"...

...."Your dad loves you"......................

...............................I am trying to be both...

....

....

....a daughter........................

....a ghost.........................

....

In *Ghostly Matters*, Avery Gordon writes on the drive to narrate the history that hurts: "It is about putting life back in where only a vague memory or a bare trace was visible to those who bothered to look. It is sometimes about writing ghost stories, stories that not only repair representational mistakes, but also strive to understand the conditions under which a memory was produced in the first place, toward a countermemory, for the future."

....
....

To write a book is to write into a future and I am not ready.

....
....

There was a time I worked so much I couldn't sleep. R said I was a dense bubble of worries. They pressed my body onto the bed and said, "Rest, rest," and it was like a game, how awful I was at it. I would shoot up from the bed, out of their arms. Back on the train, on the bus, to a faraway borough. I carried a suitcase with me as if I was going somewhere that was not the job and not the hive. I left too soon—the house, the bed, the quiet weight of R's couch where we were watching each other. They said, "It's like you're a stranger."

....
....
....

I don't know where this comes from.

I know exactly where this comes from.

....
....
....

We mimic the species that perform a certain ideal means of survival.

....

....

....

....

....

....

....

....

....

....

....I think it's funny that the book is not about bees at all............................

....

....

....

....

....

I wanted to write a book about Orpheus and
Eurydice, how they lived and died and died again.

How hellish, discovering that the journey was not
enough, even at its end, that impulse to look back,
which is like admitting grief is a form of self-sabotage.

....

....

....

And then she was ash.

....

....

....

....

....

....

Another myth: my father swimming from mainland China to then British occupied Hong Kong. When he was caught, he disappeared for a while into the fields. One can say he worked there and discovered the body as an ox that could keep on even if

....

....

the migration as a broken history

....

....

we don't talk about

....

....

....

How do you write a history that is both [yours] and [not yours] but an extension of an improbable future?

..................in which the girl writes the book...

....to become subject by way of sharing.................

....the labor......a movement...............

....................into this future of unknowns......what language we are making with our bodies.................

....with work.......................with hard work.........

The story of labor is that it goes on.

The hive hums its vacant sound.

In the comb, the honey is slow and its obedience bruises me.

Noise falls out, a frailty of many cells.

My father, inside a cylinder of white smoke, was an efforted *alive*.

He became harsh as a tyrant bell.

I swear love is a hollow tomb.

And the rest of us—we carried him; we were the tomb.

"I heard it from mom who told it, and can you tell it again?"

"Is it work if it doesn't hurt? If you like it?"

"Are you allowed to like it? The work?"

"If it hurts and you are not sure if you like it, is that also work?"

For a while not saying [   ] because it was bad form

....

....

....

My father had been complaining about a possible ulcer.

....

He ignored most pains as he was accustomed.

....

....

....

....

....

....

The book leaves out this story, which contains gold and tulle and other objects not frequently featured in narratives of [   ] or witness:

On the night before my senior prom, attempting to finesse the zipper of my gold mermaid dress that had stopped halfway up my torso, I was using an ineffective combination of coat hanger, paper towel, and butter. That night, my father came into my room. He told me that he had less than [ ] months to live. It was [ ] and it had accelerated in his body. Not an ulcer but a different monster. He sat on my bed and let the words hang stale in the air. I folded twenty times into his lap—the zipper on my side without any give—a gush of gold and tulle scattered across the wooden floor.

………

The next day, I danced into the dawn, shimmering in a devastation that looked and felt like a human-sized hole.

………

Later, learning that there are some bees who live alone.

………

I would tell this story years after with laughter.

………

Unsure what else to do.

………

Perhaps all of this is to suggest that the book is not enough. Or apologetically to everyone, I would say: "I'm sorry that I wrote a sad book."

....

....

....

....

....

....

....

....

....

The poet Arati Warrier in her poem "Alive" says:

"I plan to love so loudly, my body
abandons every demon harvesting me."

....
....
Let me tell you.........
.........a story which
begins with............
a death and ends......
......with a study......
of a life of labor......
.........done with such
seeming ease.........
....
It is like an art.........
the way it takes on...
......this other.........
......life the body......
as another..............
metaphor while......
also literally............
......doing...............
its job.........to write
the story.................
.....of itself the........
words lost..............
before....................
they were ever.........
......spoken but I......
suppose this is.........
......a way..............
......to remember......
.........with holes.....
....
....

THE PLURAL CIRCUITS OF TELL

The project: because no one talks about remainders, I hope to draw the line from here to there, scattering in between the points, a nominal [feeling] of what an absence looks like when dispersed.[1]

---

1. The migration of the cancer cell, otherwise known as invader of healthier and naturally growing cells within the body.

Dispersal—the distribution of animacy across a subject's once happy plane. For instance, "I was happy once," my mother said, referring to the games she would play in her youth. I played those too, the elastic thread we wrapped around our ankles, torso, neck. We leapt and we hurled our bodies through this entanglement. And then somewhere between us, a severing. Or metastasis—the cancerous cell, in its effort to become not one but many, splits and duplicates. They are called daughter cells for that reason.

"Once" is a type of beginning.[2] When I was younger, I began
every story with "Once" as a way of signaling
the singular arrangement of our time.

But in fact, it always happens more than once.
For every child wandering into the mangled
course of the woods, watched by wolves, the night
eventually comes again and again, in all the days after,
marching into a forgetting spell—nothing the lone
surviving parent says can soothe them of the eyes' slow
blink in the even slower dark.

---

2. "Once" is also recitation. The story that would not be forgotten.
In the theory of push and pull, the disproportionate histories of
political and economic intervention make it impossible for two
countries to live their lives in singularity. The intimacy of such
contact coalescing into a force. When people of one nation are pro-
pelled towards the other. A migratory impulse. A movement that
happens more than once.

My grandfather's painting of a two-story house in Guangzhou has
hung above his kitchen table for as long as I can remember, and
it remains there long after his death. I feel that I know this house
intimately, though I have never been, and as a child, I drew poor
imitations of that image, what seemed like a dream inhabiting
another city.

When my mother returned to Hong Kong in 2007, she and I made
plans to visit this house. At the restaurant where my uncle and
mother had just finished their last pot of tea, my mother expressed
our plans to stay several nights in Guangzhou. In response, my
uncle recounted several incidents he had heard about in the news
of a roaming motorcyclist in Guangzhou who would take a length
of sharp wire and decapitate his victims as he rode past. "Times
have changed since you've lived there," he said, as if fact. In the days
following, my mother paced my uncle's apartment, going, "What do
I do? What do we do?" Then, deciding that she wanted us to keep
our heads, we never went.

Such is the potency of imagination and the ways that stories spiral.
In the case of the house, my mother never intended to return, only
wanting to see it one more time so that I would know it through
sight and touch. As for me, it was not longing I felt, but the clos-
est thing to injury against the gauntlet of history and my uncle's
mouth. His fear. His most contagious and rabid fear.

What remains to tell: the writing of this story, in this time.
How I replicate the narrative of myself across different spaces.

Today and every day after, I wear a pleated mask.
It was my grandmother who taught me to cut a mango,
so I eat and think of her, she who has passed a thousand times.
I wear her face, I don my mother's attire, our inheritance
like a distant thread that does not stop weaving.
In one delicate swoop, the water of my life
can fall—each splatter, a new pattern I cannot escape.[3]

---

3. There was my mother's cancer and then there was my father's. In each instance, the organ revolted, and they were sunken for a while. But the fact that my mother lives and my father died was no product of a greater cure. I began to see in each of them a cruel optimism. For Lauren Berlant, it is "the condition of maintaining an attachment to a problematic object *in advance* of its loss."

When I was a child, my parents asked me which one of them I loved the most. I only wanted to please. To my mother, I would say, "I love you most," and to my father, "But I love you the most." Each parent believing that they were recipient of the bigger love. When found out, they laughed and told the story of my cunning for years. Now, I wonder what it means to believe for a moment that my love could be any less. In the face of possible death, was my father's attachment to life propelled by a determination towards that greater love? In his passing, did he believe it to be dimmer than the nearby flame?

Once and several times after, I would forget myself
and move through my days as if a blank slate.
Then, they would call me, and it would be another
Asian woman's name.[4] Waiting there, I would turn doe
until correction, and always, the apology bears
a light touch of resentment. The plural of me
and yet they cannot tell me apart.
Says Trinh T. Minh-ha, "All is empty when one is plural.
Yet how difficult it is to keep our mirrors clean."

---

4. If the zygote is the cell that constitutes the first formation of human life, then the cancer cell is also first in its animacy. Whereas life has a certain determinism—we know exactly from where it came and where it will go—the cancer's origin and path remain unknown. At once a mystery of genetic disposition and environment, the cancer cell thwarts a linear story. Some number of factors can cause the cell to change, to become more of itself in the face of some unnamable loneliness. It may insist that it was not frightened when it began, but by populating the body as tissue, it had conquered its oneness.

Often, I remember even the things I am not supposed to remember or did not belong to me.

...

In celebration of becoming American, my parents bought a plastic tree, and in their happiest days, the angel top stood high on chopstick stilts, so eager were they to help the object remain upright.

...

In this inheritance, a sign hangs over everything: YOU TOO CAN MAKE IT IF YOU TRY.[5]

---

5. On its way to becoming cancerous, a cell first enters metaplasia, brought on by contact with an abnormal stimulus such as a chemical agent. In metaplasia, the cell changes its internal properties to adapt to its new environment. But adaptation should not be confused with assimilation. The former transforms to bear the stresses of its surroundings. The latter attempts to perform in the likeness of its external environment's demands. Something is lost in the former exchange—the cell, in mutation, becomes estranged from itself and moves forward in its life as something uncomfortably other.

I, too, think of such costs, what it means to try beyond recognition.

This was my father's face upon passing:

the air cut in so pale the veins shined bright green it was almost aquatic
swimming in that blue room where scarcely the light would enter when he
exhaled the room filled thick as a plea how often are our bodies begging
to be relieved of us he said no words [it was dawn] [the new year came in]
feverish and clean. Never had I ever seen a body work so hard at being
still.[6]

<hr />

6. Seward Park High School, the school my mother attended as a teenager shortly after immigrating to the U.S. from China, was named after William H. Seward of the Burlingame-Seward Treaty of 1868 that permitted trade between the U.S. and China. The treaty lasted for two years, granting ease of Chinese immigration to the U.S. However, the growing Chinese population was such a source of anxiety to those in the country that the Chinese Exclusion Act was passed to restrict Chinese immigration to the U.S. Incidentally, the high school is located along the fringes of New York City's Chinatown, walking distance to the garment shop where my mother and her sisters would work after school. When I pass by the old campus, I am reminded of the proximity between praise and fear, how a people can be lauded one year and then detested the next. They would build monuments out of these feelings.

And because my father never finished high school, he thought of this another way, always going about his life with some strain. I saw him once at night sitting by the windowsill, his cigarette in hand. I had with me, a pack of cards, and asked him if he wanted to play. Declining as he often did, the day's work wearing on him, he watched instead. Even in his stillness, the smoke dressed him in white.

[the haunted years]

The briar reached around the house and made it its own. Within its new architecture, the family became a band of ghosts that glowed with virtual noise. It took so much to cancel out the grieving air that I revolted against my body and became an angry race.[7] I made myself a menace, a sharper and more unforgiving thing. I threw myself against the briar edge, and it being more cutting than I, tossed me back. This would go on for years, the one constant. To be unspectered, the body must harden against itself and rush into the bludgeoning. This is all it knows and comes to portend.

---

7. As the cell enters its cancerous phases, it becomes disoriented.
Its loss known only to itself.

Somehow always returning to this impasse. I try to astral project my way out of it. Beginning with the body lying flat on the bed, elbows to the side, arms perpendicular to torso. Nodding off, the arms naturally fall, and hitting the bed, wake the body up. Done enough times, the body becomes practiced in slipping between sleep and waking. Eventually, one hopes to puncture that gap of time, to leave the body, if only momentarily, to leap up and beyond the house. Unfortunately, I have never mastered it, but developed instead, a pattern of restless sleep. Even now, I have been told I look like I am racing against myself in my dreams.

The problem: upon dispersal, the bodies proliferated in every direction, such that it becomes a type of contagion, feared as it were by these healthier bodies that will against the idea of being touched, or in this case, contaminated.[8]

---

8. Interlude: the cancerous cell en route to becoming cancerous tissue is a long-contested path, very rarely seen in its infancy. So much of what we know banks on what reveals itself in the light, the tumorous growth in the shape of a protruding lump, an organ assailing against itself. Rioting.

In health class, the teacher would show the film *Outbreak* (1995) to cover both units on hygiene and sexual education. In the film, the host species for the Motaba virus is a monkey from Zaire whose illegal transport to the U.S. leads to a series of infections among humans. Beginning once as a virus passed through fluid exchange, it acclimates to its new environment and evolves into airborne virality. Confronting the proliferating state of the virus, the U.S. government plans to decimate an entire small town in California where the disease has spread.

Though it was widely agreed that the U.S. response to the virus felt overblown, to say the least, no one anticipated that years later, the film would foreshadow the spread of a disease globally that would trigger the same suspicion of foreign elements.[9] The source of the Coronavirus, assigned to an eastward origin; it wore an Asian face behind a surgical mask, both the objects of equal fear and scorn. These too can propagate.

In the final test for health class, we were asked to determine how the lessons of *Outbreak* can be applied to our own hygienic and sexual practices. In other words, it is a danger to want. Without knowing it then, we had signed a promise to say nothing of our desires. Every expression, when spoken, would be deemed immediately deviant.[10]

---

9. Identifying the problem as such: "the diagnostic promise of the categories of life and death is itself in crisis." Mel Y. Chen argues that a compulsion towards life is how we stay locked in the idea of subjecthood. When the pursuit of life and opposition to death exist only as naturalized impulses, then we preclude the instances in which a body or bodies of people actively refute both. Such are the instances of self-immolation or other death directives meant to move beyond the container of the individual to the state, to make tangible that power that manages a life.

10. Upon being born or resuscitated against our will, the state has the audacity to say, "I am giving you your life. I am giving you *back* your life."

Still, to this day, my mother would not call remission anything except the absence of tumor. No talk of gratitude or religiosity. Though I speak of appreciation all the time—giving thanks for fresh cooked fish on the table, giving thanks she did not die.

:

In a preposterous theory to my family, after we had all contracted a cold from one another, I was remembered as having said that any family that did not get sick together must not have loved each other quite as much.[11]

---

11. An article in *The Economist* entitled "Chinese Sneezes," which speculates about the growing dominance of Chinese financial markets over the U.S., is published alongside the popularized image of an East Asian person in a surgical mask. The image of protection against contagion, which harkened back to the 2002 SARS outbreak, persists as an ever-present reminder of how disease and a people can be locked in the same imaginary configuration—as if the disease is and was a people. As it came to be upon the arrival of COVID-19. When given the chance to correct himself, U.S. President Trump insisted upon his public usage of the term "Chinese Virus" instead of its scientifically recognized name. "Because it came from China," he said, and then flimsily, "It's not racist at all." Although the mask proliferated, becoming a matter of everyday life, the association between survival of oneself and hatred for an entire people became unnecessarily bound.

Even when I am angry with my mother, I still miss the pale vibrancy of her face.[12]

In her fury too, I long to see what red terrain endures. If only to know what lies ahead for me.[13]

---

12. In metastasis, the cancerous cell has proliferated and invades tissue and other neighboring bodies. Organs that touch. The blood through rapid circulation. At its strongest, the cancerous cell can penetrate through the body's barriers. So much can be said of the contained body, and yet, the foulest cell can topple its pristine order. In various treatments, the goal of eradicating every malignant cell is an attempt to halt the spread—to expel it. To leave the body intact and without memory of it ever being there.

13. According to Teresa Brennan, the condition of late capitalism has produced an affective excess where "there is too much affective stuff to dispose of, too much that is directed away from the self with no place to go." The sanctity of the body as a contained form is no longer useful in the political demands of our time. In trying to articulate a feeling, it has already passed.

[conclusive statements]

What my father had was Stage IV pancreatic cancer, discovered at the late stage of its development. Confused for an ulcer, he had put it off, thinking it was his body's knotted revenge for years of abuse. He had survived arrest once, caught in the waters while swimming to Hong Kong where he had hoped to board a plane with his sister to the U.S. On a subway platform late one night, on the way home from work, he was mugged and stabbed in the stomach with a pocketknife—that too, he survived. It came as no surprise then that the earliest signs would register as anything but its awful truth. How the proliferation of the years can wear on a body. Unraveling towards the end of his life, he began to look like the assemblage of his many parts. He was very much afraid. In collecting him, I saw what I knew was a strange biology that willed its way across several histories without subjecthood or nation. And this: the lone cancerous cell glows the way the busiest terminal of a city fills with people in the hour of its utmost vitality.

A CAREFUL LIST OF ALL MY FAILURES

Every year, the same ritual of halving myself before each benevolent ghost

gold-flecked paper lit until its inevitable blossoming   moth, angel, ash-bead

I am reminded sometimes
the floundering can be
gentle while also singed.

Here, my body tilts forward in an eternal rocking.

There, I carried incense too far
to the south of me, the wind blew the fire out.

With such mournfulness, I was talking   I sang it deep into my bones
and clumsily the talking became a fugue   cowed for you

                                                                                                   & you

                                                                                                          &

                    I was tall as a carousel bush
                    wanting always to please

                    but my badness seeks
                    unfilial pleasure

                    discovered too early
                    how to sift
                    through my own self-loathing

                    but my body did not bow [it bent].

40

My mother calls it a "bettering" as in: "Do you think you are better than me?"

Because being bad has a texture like the rubbing together of two unlike stones.

Its spark means plenitude. It has no exact translation.

That I swallowed my words for six years until they were as rotten as me.

So, she planted a sword in herself.

And I took the sword and sunk it down my grotto.

In such variable tricks, we survived for years.

My bad made of dirt, glitter, and so much bloat.

How American, this language of ascension.

That I could spit back, "I did not ask to be born."

And mean it.

Claire Jean Kim calls it the "field of racial positions," the arrangement of different bodies along a dying field, vying for the one blade of fresh cut grass. As if none of us are fit for water.

What the theory of racial triangulation tells us is the distribution of inequities rooted in white dominance. That I could look to you and feel that I am at once lesser and perhaps fortuitous for having earned that small morsel of god.

To bend so far back, my spine becomes another flag. Of assimilable colors.

And I am not even legible to myself. Cannot not even English my way out.

At my eradication, my first love wrote me
a poem about my body, telling me
what my body was when knuckle creased,
how I knew it was a trap but could not
gather my flesh fast enough those were
the heaviest days when I was filled
with so much rain and did not know
what he meant when he said, "You are
the prettiest pretty my pretty can you
speak Japanese to me can you my pretty
please" and I was so grateful to be
even considered while dissolving
beneath him that I shuddered away
the alarm and said, "That is not me"
but also "Okay."

Some days it is so quiet it feels like begging

one day, smaller than a fingernail
another day, the colossal fury of a rising tide

in a nation of proximity and degree
what is my likeness to a thumb?
the brutal texture of my race beside another?

the history of my particulars
only a fraction of a tower

how luminous my non-speech
how my ghost becomes a hiss

the resistance lives in me, I know

though how

A history racing against itself knows only

meaning through monument   the isolation of grief in a great alone.

The way my therapist traced it: the trauma wheel [in perpetuity] moves

and comes upon a wall   smacking against its bright white surface

often on an unsuspecting day   in succession

until it begins to feel like   [a drowning].

On paper, the steely faces of my ancestors bear the mark of trying.

As in the act of striving would do the body good.

The bones buck up, refuse to lose.

The white woman who said, "I am jealous of your culture; you will never run out of things to write about."

The porous matter of one's racial suffering.

Such myths we prepare for ourselves.

In a singular language—a cleansing.

That absence can feel like relief.

Still, to my mother, I described how I wanted to live
a good life of many candied gratitudes.

I wanted to be bigger than a bruise.

So much noise, I patterned my breaking.

But my queerest self, buckling against the frame, is something other.

When R folded the sheet over me, the city was quiet and borderless. I dreamed.

Even locked within the room, I poured out of it.

Leah Lakshmi Piepzna-Samarasinha asks,
"Where is this place our baby bodies sprinted towards
even when we were holding still for as long as possible?"

In other words, what does it mean to be free?

      The sky of my love is full of tumult. That, I know.

          In the dying field, pointing to my own body,
          I saw that it was mine   was always there
          and it spoke when I spoke
          a language of two
          hardened places
          and there I lived
          despite it all.

LIFE OF A DROWNING

One winter, I stepped out of my house and planted my body in a patch of white snow. I wanted to know what it would be like to be both anvil and a green shoot. I slept there. I forged a surrender in the ground.

Though I lived, the snow grew inside me in the years to come.

...

...

...

Testing the theories of flight, I once tied scarves into a patchwork parachute, hoping to catch air as I fell. I thought it meant the body as breath, a feathering. Of floating belief.

I leapt from the tallest wardrobe, my arms spread wide. Thus, it began—the history of my obstinance. My body fell smack against the red carpet. I could assail against myself like this time after time.

What my preoccupations with dying have taught me is that my body is of me and also not. A myth made of red cardinals on a blood bed. Many have been here before. They would point to one end of me and say, *This is mine* and then another, *This is also mine.*

When I undressed, it would also be this way: They peeled off one skin and then another. Like a Russian nesting doll set, I wobbled with my various hollows when they shelled me out. There were so many hands. They were always searching, going, *Come out, come out or else we will rub you out.*

...

...

...

Your body is not yours. The path of water from one country to another is stored in the silo of my father's back breaking. There is no room for me except what I can carry too. We dive quickly into the foam of an imperfect dream. There, I wash him in a claw-foot tub. It rained incessantly then. I know this puckered body better than my own. I have held its veins like clutches of fine wire. *Take care of each other*, he says. When I touch the corner of his mouth, he dissolves into ash and never visits again.

I kiss the flooding and it kisses me back. Grief pours through me like a sieve. Its aftermath of sand and salt debris grows heavy at the banks. I kiss that too.

...

...

...

What does it mean that our lungs are 90 percent water, and yet, we are capsized every time?

French immunologist Jacques Benveniste says that water is capable of memory—the way its molecules can touch an antibody and retain its biology even long after the antibody's departure. A remarkable fact considering how water molecules' hydrogen bonds are constantly shifting. Despite water's propensity towards movement—the unstable nature of its parts—it recalls every drowning.

How the guppies got along in mourning times: In a fish tank wide as the room of our breaths, my brother swam among the scavenger fish with bright lights above his head. When he floundered, I would lift him with my back. Because we had no gills, we would bob heavily through the water, bashing against the surface.

How ready I was to give my body over despite the off-knowledge, the sick-in-the-hole feeling in the gut—I was not made for this life.

...

...

...

In an absent corridor, the water spilled out onto the floor, the silver fish leaping. How frantic they were, slapping against the linoleum. This, too, I dreamed. When I picked them up one by one, their interiors lit up—their stomachs, clots of bright pink tremors.

How do you know when something has happened? In the years to come, it waits.

Returning to the scene as one would to a crime. What crime. Guilt dangles over the corrupted space. Seized light overhead and the body keeps shrinking. What crime. He says he loves her so what crime. She makes herself flat as a lake in a windless town. Nothing moves her. Not even the red spiraling out from her in circle thread. What crime spans beyond a year and she lets it. The thread lengthens into the future and it weaves its red lining into every marrow of her life, which is now no different than criminal and the crime.

...

...

...

A thread courses through a body filled with stones, so heavy with the currents of that missing life.

I brought the color red to my mother who fashioned it into a red cloak, and I wore it so close to my person that none of me ever got out.

...

...

...

Once, when I was a jar, I invited a stranger home to rattle me. He shook and he shook. He saw that inside the jar was a city within water and the lights were bare. He placed his hand on the lid to pry the damn thing off but broke his hand. Placed his teeth on the lid's edge and shattered his jaw. When he left, I collected his broken things, which were vital to powering my city.

I threw my body to the ground. The floor sank below me. I plummeted and I knew the sea.

...

...

...

In a dream, I began to flood.

In the basement of an old house on the far edges of Queens, its windows boarded up—I was shut. Water poured out the cracks of me.

Sitting across on a little rowboat—a man in all fur, unbothered. I was in love though I knew only his purple insides. He looked at me with ecstatic doom and I knew the callousness and perfect shape of this longing. There was a dim light and he touched me there. The basement filled with water and we rose with it. Our heads touched the ceiling. Said my heart: *It is the end*. He opened his mouth and there I lived for many years after that.

I was describing to my mother the sensation of moving through my days like a runner trying to finish a marathon in a pool of molasses. I saw that the world was on fire, but I was only ready for the most immediate disaster, which was the realization that I could not swim and was sinking with painful slowness. I might have cried too. She said, *Can you manage*, and it was not a question. I told her I was a marriage of *fine* and *fine*. My sadness was not louder than her relief.

DEAR INTIMACY OF [THEORY]

Of which I make grooves in my

skirt imagining all possibilities

for wandering. These are the most

precious parts of my days. When

the forest can decamp without me,

the place fleeing the person. I want

to write these possibilities the way

trees can rush forth into its most

unknowable entanglements. Root

defying root in its bind. In a sense,

this is a love letter in which I, now

forestless, am seeking you in the

swarm. When I say [intimacy] I do

not mean that every experience
within me is forageable. I mean that
a certain care can hold the water
still enough and it is teeming with
life. In bell hooks' terms, [theory]
as "location for healing" / "theory
as intervention" makes the living
something worthy of amassing.
That is all I want. Your gratuitous
sorrows falling out a bell sleeve,
asking, *How do I repair?* Even as
your sorrows parrot other sorrows.

[theory] of a girl asleep in a hole the forest left

there were puffed up flowers and bees and webs spun out of sugarspit

all that gushed up storm, its rainy innards, departed too

in its absence, a hole where a single body fit / the body that filled it

was cycling through the third stage of dreaming in which night fell

over the vast part of her mind where another forest lived

its flowers dead and unhoneyed, the bees gave no more sugar to spiders

instead, the webs were knotted with a god's cruel design

bidding no one leave, the dream shuttering itself and the girl

in her sleep could not wake and therefore had no testimony to give

self-annihilation [theory]

Often, I'll think back on it with
some shame, the age of him and
what I coveted, which was to be
fully human and immeasurable
in regard to my gifts and talents
as a young student. My youth was
a type of chariot that yanked the
sun around with some duty of
importance I'm always forgetting.
This is the life of the institution.
For love of [theory], I read for what
the world concealed and found

myself in it. If there was any skill

I acquired, it would be that—to

locate the body even when told

it does   not   exist. In that way,

I was boundless. Then, I awoke.

A nearness to excellence could

make the blood feel clean. Rattle

the husk of me until my worthiness

felt itself begin a low-lit glow.

In truth, nothing did happen,

but then what words can I assign

this hole, to point the way there,

where no theory would ever feel

sufficient? To be plucked out of the

many, to sing that song of highest

belief, I stuffed my body's hole

with stones. Out of devotion, I

can wage such war against myself.

I MARVEL AT THE NOISES
A MORE PERFECT VENGEANCE MAKES

the unkindness of being :: when I feel my feeling warped

in the lining of a thickening wall :: the triumph of water corroding the frame

femme :: a sickle :: copper flesh inside a thorn :: within the writing

of what it means to be a body :: tired of being a body

I dream a vessel licked clean of its interior sugar.

Vision of spackle, vision of needle without consequence.

Inside me, a prescient fire is coated with warning.

Born into violation, that vast net of mourning hair.

The dead play the same song throughout my life. Two notes warbling through

twinned bodies—the pink meat of my abuser, my own slotted hide.

Geum-Ja dreams of angels inside a yellow cake.

The child is dead and the killer lives free. It has been years.

Inside a prison, the ghost does not age, a *shut up* sprite

chasing his favorite marble. Grief alchemized into its truest form.

The dead keep playing a baroque tune. Geum-Ja lights two candles.

She cannot forget. It is the perpetual season of snow and ash.

What is fairness but an ounce of my meat?
In the law of the world, a single narrative is sutured clean.

How do you tell a cauterized wound not to confront the harming body?
I remember everything before and after and nothing in-between.

Does my fury also receive its right to dream?
The systems in which I place my whole life shudder against my waking.

When Geum-Ja dreams of the man who shuttered her life away,
she pictures hauling him through a field in a wooden sled.
Our fears can turn us deer-like. The man, bound hoof to hoof, looks up at his captor.
In fantasies, revenge can have this pastoral grace. His trembling animal. Her delight in his trembling.

the container, a mercy filling :: this genre of excess :: gelatinous plea ::

supposing I once was that lonesome deer in the forest growing a hunted wound ::

victimed :: survived :: generations in a vining rot :: men after men in the knife-like

stagger of time :: years the violence perfected :: a forever crest :: the opposite of a life

The ornate quality of revenge: my metal forged through half a lifetime of planning.

Sometimes a perpetrator is a tower, incapable of apology.

Sometimes his thriving diminishes the patterning of his harm.

The man keeps dangling tokens of his victims on a cellphone chain.

Where the voices of the dead are tiny bells.

A femme spy passes a note to another.

The pages assembled into a scheme.

We who have been listening all along.

I give you this flower for you have vengeance to take, comrade.

Geum-Ja is sorry three times:

The tale of complicity. When I must acknowledge my part in the brutal making of this flower. A sheep wearing a wolf's bite. I was afraid once too. Please forgive me. I could not see the sharpness of your pain. I tended too diligently to my own.

The tale of regret. When I must take leave of my body, which no longer imagines a future for itself. I left you there. In the room that continues sinking. I have only the memory of a bell. How I forsake you there too.

The tale of revenge. When I must make myself into a weapon to right it. *Atonement, do you understand?* In my error, a silken loss. When the law fails, my heart must become harder than a bullet. I dare not quake at the sound.

Geum-Ja plans a birthday party:

The families look on. The blanket horror on the screen, the sheet white of their faces. For once having thought they could not go on, and now—a resurgence of purpose. The man in the next room. His face, a taut line. The courts have absolved themselves of any further doing beyond a faulty verdict. A decision made. Then the howl. They cannot bear it, the mourners. The children were already dead when weeping.

.

.

.

I blame myself. My devotion to a word I thought was pristine. I wanted to be a body that could figure itself clean. Wanted in this way, corded through someone else's design. Something has been taken and it does not matter what. My quiet sense of aftermath? The eager pacing of time? I turn a corner and I cannot breathe. I paint the shadows between my legs. What lamb resides there, bleating and alone in a field? It is not safe for you, for us. I know that now by the nighttime blade.

.

.

.

Silence in the other room as the families rage on, a deep red pummeling. A pool of him in a plastic sheet, swimming in a non-apology.

When told to access a higher feeling, the reverse crowning of vengeance, do I just laugh? The too muchness of a stirring. How often one is told the injury is not enough. The loud pink of a judgmental thumb. How to say: I just want some peace, is all.

.
.
.

Gathering by the sweet round, the families light the candles. If they listen closely, they can hear the passing angels. There is a hush when the ghosts take flight.

There is no joy in the after.

Like everything else, the film also ends.

Geum-Ja places her face inside a tofu block.

Her daughter, witness to this long cord of shame.

The deed is done, but life goes on.

The cart of loss proceeds ahead, unthwarted by the cause.

Nothing to stuff the mouth of its redemption cry.

A ghost is still a ghost even when it finds its everlasting body.

I am sorry three times:

The tale of regret. As ghost, everything waits in the lot of *afters*. The ash of my life sits in a white cup, forever waiting its turn. Even after vengeance taken, the lanterns of our bodies stalk the streets with a vibrant hum.

The tale of regret. I pour myself into an empty field, and the grass ignites. I address the heavens with my hands, its lines wet with salt and blood. Nothing. I heave myself against a wall. The silence of birds. The remainders.

The tale of regret. Will my future life remember? Do I bear it then? And how much, the bearing.

I dream my ancestors alive, willing them to the table. How the thread of harm extends both ways.

The lining of my flesh remembers a once allegiance to a court. To be disloyal to the frame.

The vengeance outliving me. The vengeance, a persistent song.
(I can go on. I have this gift of time. From the caverns of a war, I wait.)

WHEN I IMAGINE ALL THE POSSIBILITIES
OF THE SWARM

Suppose we try to make a house of snow
and failure. In the light, the violence glows
translucent as a cellophane bark. The generations
staggered along a line. I tap along the window frame,
the ice pricking me back. The pail of us collecting water
from above in its slow drip. It runs cold like this for years,
neither one of us suspecting.
      And this is how it happens:

Each day of his youth, my father checked the cannister of rice,
watching the levels dip.   He labored.   Hunger bore a hole through him.
To each member in his family, he fed. He was so small
when his unborn sister began—a fine grain
in the womb that would not feed / would only take.
He told my grandmother, *Remove her*. For the sake of rice
and the brittle rib. My grandfather made his fists sing
into my father's face.

But this is not the beginning. Before this, two cells collided
in the early waters of a more humid time.
And before this, the universe was the kernel
of many vengeful gods.   *Before, before.*
If only to go back, to place the blame there.
The plankton's wrath. The roach and the sea.

Through the layers of sky, a pinprick narrow of sun
     burns through the glacial walls. So much water
          we cast ourselves out and out. The house to follow, a pooling brick.

        I take your hand. I plunge us into the snow.
        Whatever impressions we make will become true in its time.

Suppose the sky is flushed with change and it is possible.
The dead and the half-alive, clamoring over the stuttering
movements of speech. The wheels of our perpetual organs keep on
spinning in defiance of death's persistent volume.

Supposing it is true that when my mouth presses against the light,
there is a soft black bloom. God has no dominion over blackness.
In nature, where every color spools. I have been kissing a velvet moon.
The light bounces off the chrysalis of night mourning,
revealing an amorphous sheen.

If my father is not a ghost and my mother is not a ghost,
then I too—a maker, a shapeshifter. Bless this under-layer of sky
and its many faces. The rain is not a light poison.
There is no recourse for the things we have done to one another
when we were hurting. I suppose myself into a whorl.

When she wakes up from the solemn years, she will turn to him
and say, "Hello, the not-me." He too will wake to declare, "Hello, my courage."

Suppose my father awoke and the corners of the blue room beamed forth
with a new aliveness. In my hands, his legs grew full and supple as an apple.
He touched his toes to the ground, surprised by his sudden quickness.
The cancerous wound, a patched-up hole in the ground.

Around his bed, he ran several laps, then leapt once towards the ceiling,
the lightning coursing through him. Never mind the coldness
of the floor's linoleum—he skidded down the hall in bare feet, buckling
with laughter over the pancreatic humor of his life.
Ha ha ha rattled the hospital metal fleeing their tray.

Through every corridor, doctors and nurses clapped their hands
and touched the wing of his back. He pelted through each floor so fast,
he rose from the ground, suspended in mid-air.

The fluorescent light glowed pink as the inside of a nail.
As my father made the next furious turn, I thought,
Please don't pedal forward without me.

The gap in his hospital gown exposed a tiny sliver of a star
of which I held on. Every room in his body flooded
with the aquatic luminance of night.

When I was born, we spoke often of flight. He touched
my mother's stomach, and within her, I felt my own cord.
Thus, we began the circuitry of love and tumorous ache.

He could hurt us there and there. I watched the angels of his violence
rise from him like a tuft of yellow smoke. And there it went.
And with apology, he would live for forty more years.

Suppose I got into the car with my mother and we just drove.
The day that she left, the air filled with a prickling sound.
In the car's silver interior, we were pulled by streetlights
and the debris of night. It became possible to drink
one another's pains. Then dawn arrived.
We had crossed two state lines, waving to their soft tracks in the air.

At a road stop diner, we ate little and talked about our disappointments.
Had it not been for the kindness of apples, then what?
My great-grandmother filling the hunger of my mother,
my mother before me, my palm opening to receive.

The family women, three generations deep, sat watchfully in the corner booth.
Their mouths, a pile of salt. It was not that she regretted the quality of our births,
my mother said. But what would it be like to be chosen first and only?

I begged her to return. I begged. There are animals who study grief for years.
Did you know that, mom? I said. It was possible she heard me
and chose instead to contemplate the sugar spilled across the counter.
Each granular speck, a patterned loss. I wet it with my thumb.

How could we not see it? Our mouths brimming with action and consequence.
My father's heart turned away from us, dreaming into another future of glass.
I share my mother's face, after all. The music repeats.
Just one more hour, she said. She took my hand.
With the women, our pockets lined with sugar. We left.

Suppose it is easy to believe. Every sparrow landing leaves
a fossilized mark. The hard air pushing against its wings,
having shape, texture, and fold. Easy to swallow

what we cannot see, what the barriers of flesh cannot know.
The coarseness of evidence, the fabric of my hide.

There would be no question of feathers, their lightness accruing iron.
No animal testifying to the grave.

When I bleed, I bleed. The forest rushes to bind the body red to me.

Easy to make amends out of water. The fish leap
from the foam, and this can be a victory too.

Though I once placed too much faith in brute and ardor,
it is softness that touches me. Even in the absence of love,
I kneel before the altar of its loss, my belief lit by candle alone.

I have this belief in the afterlife of many tender objects,
the persistence of their kin. Belief that though the truth pockets holes,
I peer through blinds, and the kite of it
is waiting there with tri-colored bells.

There is proof enough for you and me. There would never be any need
for proof again. When I say, *I believe you*,
I mean this—the kite, the colors, the clarity of bells.

Suppose everybody I ever loved made up a tiny universe
in which each one thrived in their own planetary hues.
I mistook each one for the central star—common mistake.
And still, I draped each of them in the garment of changing seasons.
How many moons? I asked. They answered and I supplied.
The universe moved in strident form, each planet missing
the other in orbit. I did not intend to collapse the blue planet,
still unfurling in its newness, but the layers of its life saw no future for water.
I abandoned a dry well, I floundered. Years ago, the universe held a pale sun.
It struck a match through every star-kissed body, and in its stillness,
was painful as glass. I thought falling in love meant *white-hot*
but that was only a fraction of the universe, of time.
I felt the shadow first when I pleaded, *Eclipse me.*
It was the chaos of spurs and it burned. It came and went
and in returning, begged the spun miracle of rings.
There would be no end to this carrying.
For them, I knew I would always wait.
Turning my body over, I saw the universe was halved,
its noisy assemblage sliding towards collision.
I held the planets close. I pressed their gaseous swarms
to raucous mass. I did this so they would believe me.
Having endured the labor of the current, the universe
was fast expanding—it needed to fold. Even I could not bear it.
I surrendered, and I loved them all.

Suppose the impact was a bell, a warning instead
moving through a hollow factory. The violence of men
and the colonial rituals of their pasts were a lesson.

In the pedagogy of grief, the earth was good,
and then history, the stalwart chemicals of its wake,
still seeps in the soil. Would we not reverse that too if we could?

The atomic weight of him pressed so deep into my torso
that generations after would feel the soreness of ribs.

Suppose my grandfather never struck my aunt
because her cheek was there, and my father,
in his piety to the self-same heaving, did not instead
tell her to move out of the way.

Because I was born witnessing, and in my queerness, still desire
the love of these masculine injuries, I listened too closely
and was lost. The pattern undulates and recedes.

Suppose I became the sound of windchimes
crashing into the ground, startling the other body there
that would not move.

The ghost of my future visits my past and tells her, *You have to be brave*.
I could fortify my life this way.

My allegiance to the bone, its refusal as instruction,
will buoy me when memory is not enough.

To feel even now, the soft impressions of many thumbs.
They are not the violence I remember.
There is nothing left to forgive.

Suppose there is an end to our suffering. Like a chariot,
the absence of grief circles us with the obstinate heat
of the largest star. To believe in the radiant orbit of this fire.
To face an empty cup and find the constellated mire of you
and me and the toppling of a century. We rise from the painful
corridors of a life. Rarely did we dream of planetary rings,
and yet, tilting ourselves up, we see the heavenly bodies
of all that has passed, each one bright with surrender.
We can go on. We can dress ourselves in the celestial cloak
of this wide expanse, every woman and femme and the disorder
of the peal. I will never write another elegy again.
I am looking at you now in the acceleration of time.
All the possibilities of the swarm ignite. The humming of many
wings amassing into a greater noise. We can write our origins
sacred here and renounce the country of our fear.
There is only our singular pulse when we fill the sky.

NOTES

With gratitude to the following literary journals and anthologies for publishing previous versions of work that appear in this book:

"This is to live several lives," *Nat.Brut*
"The Plural Circuits of Tell," *Jaded Ibis Press* blog
"A Careful List of All My Failures," *Black Warrior Review*
"Life of a Drowning," *Poor Claudia*
"dear intimacy of [theory]" and "self-annihilation [theory]," *wildness*
"I Marvel at the Noises a More Perfect Vengeance Makes," *REFILL: An Anthology in Decolonial Ekphrasis*
"Suppose it is easy to believe..." and "Suppose the impact was a bell..." (from "When I Imagine All the Possibilities of the Swarm"), *Foglifter*

The work in this collection references several artists, writers, cultural workers, and scholars to whom I'm indebted:

In "This to live several lives," I quote a passage from Avery Gordon's *Ghostly Matters: Haunting of the Sociological Imagination*. I also quote a line from Arati Warrier's poem, "Alive."

In "The Plural Circuits of Tell," I cite from Trinh T. Minh-ha's *Woman, Native, Other*, Lauren Berlant's *Cruel Optimism*, Mel Y. Chen's *Animacies: Biopolitics, Racial Mattering, and Queer Affect*, and Teresa Brennan's *The Transmission of Affect*.

In "A Careful List of All My Failures," Claire Jean Kim's concept of the "field of racial positions" comes from her article, "The Racial Triangulation of Asian Americans," published in the journal *Politics & Society* in 1999. The work also features a line from Leah Lakshmi Piepzna-Samarasinha's *Bodymap*.

"dear intimacy of [theory]" references concepts from bell hooks' *Teaching to Transgress*.

"I Marvel at the Noises a More Perfect Vengeance Makes" is an ekphrastic work based after Park Chan-wook's *Lady Vengeance* (2005). Geum-Ja is the name of the female protagonist who was falsely imprisoned for 13 years after a child murderer, who also happened to be her former teacher, forced her to confess to a crime she did not commit. During her incarceration, she plotted her revenge against the real child murderer and executed the plan upon her release from prison with the help of other recently released inmates. In the film's conclusion, she gathers the family members of the deceased children and allows them to exact vengeance upon the murderer as they deem fit. The essay in verse features dialogue from the film, which include the statements in English, "I give you this flower for you have vengeance to take, comrade" and "Atonement, do you understand?"

ACKNOWLEDGEMENTS

First and foremost, I would like to thank Fei Chin, Wai Mo Leung, and Kent Leung for being the first family in my life. Thank you as well to the women in my family across the generations. You have made all this writing possible, and I hope these words do justice to the complexity of our experiences.

Thank you to my dear mentor, friend, and some-times uncle, Truong Tran, for lending me space to write, create, and explore without fear. At night sometimes in your studio, I would turn on all the light sculptures and feel the swarm ignite within me.

I finished this book during my residency at Blue Mountain Center where I am so grateful to have benefitted from the deep reading and advice towards this manuscript from Denice Frohman, Kalima Young, Rachel Kauder Nalebuff, and Elizabeth Brina. My deepest appreciation to Iddo Aharony for inspiring this book's title with his tale of fireflies lighting the way and for his enduring friendship. I am especially grateful to Thomas, Sara, Kei, Intaba, and all the staff of Blue Mountain Center for taking such good care of us and our art.

A special thanks to David St. John and the writ-ers at his poetry workshop who had the oppor-tunity to read the first draft of this book. I am especially indebted to the kindness and support of Catherine Pond and Katie Ogle.

Thank you to the literary spaces and editors who have either published excerpts of this book or offered time for the work to thrive. This includes the wonderful staff at the Sundress Academy for the Arts, *Foglifter*, *wildness*, *Black Warrior Review*, Alyssa Manansala, Rosa Boshier, Yanyi Luo, Stacey Tran, and others named here.

My eternal gratitude to my best friend Kati Barahona-Lopez whose commitment to justice and building a better world inspires me constantly to both critique and hold open the possibility for transformation. Without your belief in me all these years, this book would not have happened.

To Vanessa Angélica Villarreal, my first and forever friend in Los Angeles, thank you for helping me grow my poetic voice, to write with heart and blood, to allow this work to be expansive. How can I ever thank you enough for teaching me to be brave?

Thank you, Ica Sadagat, for allowing me to be as I am without shame or judgment. I steered this book as my most fortified self, and always, you were there to remind me that I have openness to spare.

This book would not have been possible without the support of my frequent collaborator Matt Orenstein who witnessed this project at its very start. Thank you for everything.

I am indebted to the friendships of so many, but I am especially grateful for the care, humor, and intellectual challenge from the following: Gustavo Barahona-Lopez, Veronica Garcia, MT Vallarta, Dan Lau, Tiana Nobile, Cathy Linh Che, Saretta Morgan, Christina Olivares, Chen Chen, Will Giles, Kay Ulanday Barrett, Addie Tsai, Angela Peñaredondo, Luke Rampersad, SA Smythe, Jean Ho, Kenji Liu, Vickie Vertiz, Soraya Membreno, Xochitl-Julisa Bermejo, Ashaki Jackson, Neela Banerjee, Jen Hofer, Leesa Fenderson, Lauren Eggert-Crowe, Douglas F. Brown, Andrea Gutierrez, Cherisse Yanit Nadal, Jordan Nakamura, Emily Jungmin Yoon, Michelle Lin, Kazumi Chin, Jennifer S. Cheng, Janice Lobo Sapigao, Sally Wen Mao, Claudia Leung, Kyle Chu, mai c. doan, Phuong Vuong, Shelley Wong, Monica Sok, Ching-In Chen, Celeste Chan, Angie Sijun Lou, Rachelle Cruz, Lisa Marie Rollins, Mushim Ikeda, Reed Brice, Michael Wasson, Sarah Clark, Naima Yael Tokunow, Patricia Tolete, Abigail Devora, Kimberly Jones, Jacquelyn Grant Brown, and JD Scott.

My love to Kundiman founders, Joseph Legaspi and Sarah Gambito, for forging the path with such visionary and fiercely loving leadership.

To my VONA/Voices Writing Workshop family, thank you for inspiring in me to believe in a more radical future—T.K. Lê, Jacqueline Barnes, Stefani Cox, Nia Hampton, Maya Beck, Joseph Earl Thomas, Ariel Eure, Rosana Cruz, Aaron Talley, LaTanya Lane, Junauda Petrus-Nasah, Laura Villarreal, Esther Choi, Tina Zafreen Alam, John Hyunwook Joo, Zeyn Joukhadar, Danielle Buckingham, and Ruben Miranda.

Through the years, *Apogee Journal* has been an instrumental force in my education as a poet and editor, and now has become another family. Thank you, Alex Watson, Mina Seckin, Joey De Jesus, Zef Lisowski, Crystal Yeung, Crystal Hana Kim, Brian Lin, Legacy Russell, Anya Lewis-Meeks, Alejandro Varela, Arriel Vinson, Ingrid Pangandoyon, Stine Westergaard, and Miriam Kumaradoss. And to those who are no longer with *Apogee* but continue to thrive brilliantly—Cecca Ochoa, Denne Michele Norris, and Safia Jama.

My gratitude to Noemi Press who published my first book, *Bone Confetti*, especially to Carmen Giménez Smith, Suzi F. Garcia, Diana Arterian, and Sarah Gzemski for helping me believe in my ability to make a book, for believing that I have something special to share.

Thank you to everyone at Nightboat Books for guiding me through my second book, for helping me continue this journey.

Lastly, thank you to Dr. Susan Hammoudeh whose wisdom and counsel over the years have brought me back to myself. I am forever grateful.